MW00334811

More Blessed Than Me

JESSE: Volume 1

LA Harris

A Collection of Poetry

Journey, Exacerbate, Spirituality, Sovereignty, Ecstasy

Dare to Bear Fruit

More Blessed Than Me: JESSE Volume 1
Copyright © 2021 LA Harris

All rights reserved. Except as permitted under the U.S. Copyright Act of 1976, no part of this book may be reproduced, distributed, or transmitted in any form or by any means, including photocopying, recording, or other electronic or mechanical methods, without the prior written permission of the publisher, except in the case of brief quotations embodied in critical reviews and certain other noncommercial uses permitted by copyright law.

Although every precaution has been taken to verify the accuracy of the information contained herein, the author and publisher assume no responsibility for any errors or omissions. No liability is assumed for damages that may result from the use of information contained within.

Illustrations by Abraham Yousuf.
Cover design by Abraham Yousuf.
Editing and book formatting by Pen & Pad Publishing.

Printed in the United States of America
ISBN 978-1-7376597-0-9 (pbk)
ISBN 978-1-7376597-1-6 (hcv)

Dare To Bear Fruit
Charlottesville, VA

http://www.DareToBearFruit.com
LAH@daretobearfruit.com
/daretobearfruit
/daretobearfruit
/daretobearfruit

Dedication

To my parents, Charles William and Barbara Ann Harris...

Love never dies ... it transcends space and time.
They will be like a tree planted by the water
that sends out its roots by the stream.
Love and miss you always!

Introduction

As a child, I loved to dance! I lived in my ballet, tap and toe shoes. The joy of bare feet pressing into the dance floor, moving in step with the beats and rhythms of African, blues and jazz music as it engulfed the room. The spirit one with the music, and the body one with the motion. Dancing took me to great highs and taught me to bear various levels of pain. It has always been about movement and flow.

Until writing this book, I never realized how intertwined movement from dance and writing were as forms of expression for me. In my poems, prose, scripts and short stories, it is the sound of God's voice speaking to my spirit. When in rhythm, I am connected to a gift where words build pathways. My pathways flow with pen and paper, keyboard and computer, voice and video, embracing the hopes, fears, aspirations and belief that my dreams beckon me.

More Blessed Than Me: JESSE is an invitation to "dance" with me, an invitation to see me along with the vulnerability and courage required to let you in. You are invited to move through the pages of my life filled with great joy, devastating pain, heartbreak and heartache, family, sisterhood, love, sex, courage and the faith required to live a more enriched life on purpose.

My first prayer is that your heart, body and mind accept the invitation and find connection, feel redemption, release pain, celebrate life, question beliefs and behaviors, and realize each of us is so very blessed.

The five pathways in this book are subtitled, JESSE. These pathways ignite and birth a life forged on love, perseverance, wrestling with self-worth, disappointment, victory and faith. The pathways include **Journey**, establishing my path and its guiding light; **Exacerbate**, requiring introspection and an ability to wrestle with the impact and responsibility we have for and on the lives of other people; **Spirituality**, delving into our relationship with our Creator and the pilgrimage our souls are on prior to their crossing; **Sovereignty**, speaking to the freedom and exhilaration inherit in walking into our purpose; and **Ecstasy** as it roars with simple caresses to explosions of sensuality, reminding us of our holistic human existence.

My second prayer is that this invitation empowers you to reflect on your life and realize, given your path, who is more blessed than you?

My third and final prayer is that you feel the struggle and the courage required for me to be vulnerable. Accepting my vulnerability gave me courage in the face of shame and power, and the safety to outgrow my box so I could be in greater service to others and share this collection of poems.

Our JESSEs are powerful! Life is an education we keep giving our soul so when the music stops and our feet no longer walk an earthly path, your words... my words... these words... continue to flow.

More Blessed Than Me is a collection of 88 writings hoping to incite, influence, inspire and galvanize people in celebration of each other's purpose. Writing is my purpose. I learned being vulnerable, embracing my path, becoming comfortable with being uncomfortable and moving forward are the hallmarks to the instruments delivering *More Blessed Than Me*.

Table of Contents

Journey

Travel or passage from one place to another; movement and flow

The first poem I wrote was for Girl Scout Camp. It was called, *Camp Goodbye.* Everyone had to contribute and all I knew was to write. Standing beneath trees, moon shining bright and stars blanketing the sky, I closed my eyes and asked God to speak to me. I wanted to let everyone know how impactful that week was on my life. I wanted to say thank you, recognize the experience, wish all well, and create hope for the future.

Thus began the journey where WORDS would roll from my head, heart and soul to my "pen." As I write, the goal of a little girl on campgrounds has continued to capture the fabric of my writing for more than forty years. These gifted WORDS highlight life experiences, accomplishments, failures, questions, fears, love won and love loss, death, injustice, the "isms" (race, sex, etc.), fantasy, sex, celebrations and loss for others, and existing in this world as a daughter, a woman, a woman of color and all the labels the world placed upon us that can empower or box us in.

Take this Journey with me and may the WORDS dance from my Spirit and into your Soul!

CALLED ME TO THIS PLACE

Lord,
You called me to this place
Not in my comfort,
not part of my visual vision
but there is a reason

Going to walk
Forward
Backwards never been in my
vocabulary
But I remember
standing - sitting
still
not feeling
my joy
my anger
my dreams
my heart
My disappointment
wrapping its legs
around me,
just humping
and humping
feverishly,
trying to get
me
her
him
they
them
to give me
something

Believing
but dancing with
the fear
that nothing
will change
No one will see
me

left out
and left behind,
'cause humping
takes your eyes off the
prize,
humping
keeps your head down
your mouth
slightly parted
breathing erratic
legs tight
body engaged
brain - no focus

Calling me
to this country place
where the pace
lovingly
reduces,
maybe will eliminate
humping
moving forward
Picking this destination
knowing its far
from final
Excited about
the new rhythm of my life
beats higher
than humping
more powerful than thumping
going to new levels
everything is now
"jumping"

TIMELESS SPACE

When the moon dances through
the window
across the land of
history and families long gone,
it is the pathway to
to hearts unknown

How much love filled this land
How much joy
has the earth absorbed
Who called to us
from the future
through the moon
that once shined so bright
upon them

In this timeless space
where the sun
rises
in the same place,
how does history unfold

How have hearts been broken,
lives been changed
where sweat and equity
moved earth
and heaven claimed names

So timeless space
gives humble rest
to the hearts
that love the land
So the moon will shine
and the sun will rise
and flowers bloom
again

WHEN I WAS LITTLE (LEFT BEHIND)

When I was little
I remember thinking
if my parents die
then we all have
to go together

One could not
live long
without the other
and I could never
choose,
never wanted to
lose one,
left with the other

Package deal
the three of us,
no one else
could we trust

All the secrets
the pain
the joy
and the stains
stayed within our walls

So how dare you
leave me behind with
no encouragement or voice,
no words to read,
little choice

I was left behind
when I had no idea

Running
running
running
to exist,
not to really be here

Always running,
too much going on
to slow down
Just wanted to
be in -
included in the sound
of love
of faith
of family
of truth

Left behind
to discover
my truth

So You Offer to Help

So you offer to help
and at the first
moment of being a real help
you scream,
"I need my money back"

I could and should be
upset
but it actually caused
me to laugh

I ceased having expectations
a long, long time ago
I stopped believing in
what you said
because your actions
demonstrated the complete opposite

Funny
how you judge others
who were less than kind
to me
You may have been
sad
but it really made
you feel better
about you

So here we are,
there you are,
and all that was said
rings true
But you can't hurt me
and I can't be
disappointed,
those emotions
no longer exist

You
taught
me
well

What Does Family Mean

What does family mean?
What does faith and
following God's teaching
really mean?

Extending kindness
Extending faith and self
Dealing with births
Grappling with death
Tears and sadness
Joy and pain

Family
balances the truth
of the group
And the masks of the individuals
sometimes crying to be
who God intended
But stuck
in the skin
of the kin
born in

God's Word
asks if you
"Done did your best?"
Is the love of Christ
permeating from your
head, heart and chest?
Not the superficial
so folks can say
"You so kind"
Instead
standing up for one another
Leaving
selfishness and judgments
to rot in the
blood line

Colossians 3:13 says
"Bear with each other and
forgive one another ...
Forgive as the Lord forgave you"
Limit your perception
of perfect or
Christ like
For family
there is always room
to be compassionate
to be inclusive
to bridge the gap
to avoid using
emotional and financial
violence

Family means faith
Where love and justice
find peace and opportunity
Freedom to let Go and Let God
Prayerful enough
to carry Wednesday's Bible study
and Sunday's sermon
through the fullness of the week
Through to the Soul of
every family member

You did not create them
You are only asked to love them
Just remember
God is watching you
He sees what takes place
in your home
Exchanges on your phone
Thoughts when you are all alone
And on social media
when keystrokes are going strong

Words matter
Memories hold court
Choose God's Words

LIGHT

Light
Find me
in the darkness,
don't let it
take me away,
don't let it
keep me
from
my truth
my destiny

Light
Be my passage way
home
My spirit knows no better place,
trace
the light
that I carry
in my heart
called home

JUST BELIEVING IN VICTORY

Just believing
in my victory,
don't seem like
one is possible

The videos tell me
it's my mind;
my therapist
says it's my emotions;
my clock
says I'm running
out of time

This the best
I got?
Does it rhyme?

Believing this is a
train station,
my stop
before my destination
Help me avoid
procrastination,
all "ills"
or discourse
which keeps
minds on
the plantation

Just believing
it's all better,
right to the
bitter end

Got to believe
'cause I pray to
wake-up

Start believing
all over again!

BROKEN GLASS

The pieces of
shattered glass
reflect the various
stages and events
of my life

The size of shard does not matter
The glass it just
shattered
and each piece
has a story of its own

The piece with three points
where light dances
from the edge
reflects a life and a love
and a heart that once pledged
to be true to one
who stimulated my mind,
inspired and motivated me
and kept my legs
entwined

Mystery of romance
in each light
dances
to the rhythm of my
heart and
broken glass chances

The piece so tiny
where red
and danger meet
represents the most
potential
for pain and retreat

You barely see it
but it is ever present

ever real
for its purpose
is to linger
and your body
memory to not heal

Yet the beauty
in being broken
is the gift
of being whole
and all those
pieces
are
light to
my
Soul

FUTURE

Today,
I climbed up
the Mountain
and saw my future

I looked over
and saw
all of God's
blessings
and watched
them
Shift

I am being
Intentional
and He is
Sifting
Me

So God can use me
So His Will
is
My Way

I feel greatness
so I write
Greatness
I see my dreams
and He
protects
them from harm's way

Not too fast
Not too slow
but
guided and girded
the world
need not
know

CAME FOR ME

How you came
for me

Moved my pain
around,
not needing to
know everything

Planted my future
in solid ground

Giving words to
legacy,
something
He
formed in me

Giving words
to my cape
a destiny,
life is
about
to
unawake!

Words II

Living
Breathing
In a poem
In a rap
all of rhyme
upper case
lower case

Words

See them
Cover me
Laugh
Cry

Excited
Scared
Thinking
Believing
There is a chance,
second chance
for
Me
to find,
invent
in the
Trust
of
Me!

For Dad ... Because He Came

When you saw my dad
You saw love
Love for his family
Friends
Students
And even those who did not
Understand him or value him
Had to respect him
He is one of God's true
Foot Soldiers
Fighting for fairness and equality
Fighting for the dignity of all people
Young or old

When you saw my dad
You saw laughter
His heart was big
And his arms wide enough for all

Dad, mom and I
Called ourselves the
Three Amigos
"Through thick and thin ... we go through it together"
Needless to say a wife and her husband have a
Journey that only they share
Yet, I have them both in a special way
Wonderful parents
My dad is my hero...
My mom, my "shero"

Mom and I were blessed
For we were there
When God took him
Home to rest
And though life on earth
Will never be the same
We are a better family
Elizabeth is a better city
And the world a richer place
Because He came

SHE GAVE LOVE - MOM

Words don't
do her justice
They never ever will
Everything I start to write
brings tears and the pen goes still
What do you write
about your rock and your shield
What words best exemplify
her grace, dignity, beauty
Her heart...
She Gave Love

My father and I
were most blessed
to have a wife and mother in our corner
She Stood Up for Us
She Stood by Us
She would Stand in Front of Us,
take the brunt for us
Always there
Always protecting
Always...
She Gave Love

I miss her
I miss her
laughter,
smile,
telling stories,
jokes and her wisdom on life
I miss her presence
Heaven received an angel and my dad his wife
She Gave Love

75 years of elegance and style
Seems so long but feels like a little while
What does a daughter say
when part of her heart

has taken flight,
when what was
will no longer be
When there was once
The three Amigos,
Then the two Partners,
Now me

I can close this with
Great Faith
that as I held her hand to say goodbye,
the God she loved and thanked
had his arms opened wide
to say what only He can say
"Well done, Barbara!" as God watched from above,
delivering His greatest commandment
to her family,
friends and community
She Gave Love!

Mom and Dad

MAY THEIR HEARTS AND
COMMITMENTS TO THEIR
COMMUNITY CONTINUE TO
LIVE IN THE HEARTS AND
MINDS OF THOSE THEY
TOUCHED!

YOU WILL TELL

You will tell
me to come
To change the
direction of my life

To move to a
place
where my comfort
is in question

Where I have to
trust you
Where
for all my life
I trusted
me
me
me
Didn't know how
to do it another way

Painful choices
hear me teaching
change,
choices
Run to it!

You will tell
me to come
I will want
to go
Reach out to me

WHOLE ME

Can you love me?
Really the whole
of me
To sit in
my shit
and know
it stinks
but love me
in it,
through it,
in spite of it

To believe and bask
in the curve of
my body,
the question in my mind
Can you love me?
Not from perfection
'cause we running out of time

To sit in my majority
to find a truth
only you know

Can I love you
past your fear?
Unleash
yourself,
unwrap the harness
covering up
your soul
your choice
your voice
Let it be exposed
so I can love you

Beyond the doubts
that

hold you
hostage,
it ain't our stink
that separates us
That's weak,
easy,
low hanging fruit
to grasp
It's the question
and
the answer to

Can you,
Can I
have
the will
the desire
the fortitude and longitude
the staying power to
Love

BREAK FREE

For family and friends who lost people they love

I don't recall
our last words
and as a
New Year
attempts to break
free
my heart hesitates,
knowing that
I will only have
the essence of
who you
were - are
to me

I survived
another holiday
with your absence
and you would be
proud
how I did
my best
to honor your memory
and continue
living my life
yet
as a New Year
attempts to
break
free,
my hands hesitate
because the whole
of who I am
remembers what
it was like to be
held in your arms
when I cried
and when I celebrated

SOMEWHERE ON THIS JOURNEY

Somewhere on this journey
You said a kind word
You hugged me
You gave me encouragement
You laughed with me ... at me
You shined the love and light
of God
into my heart
and I lived longer
and better
for being blessed with
your presence

Somewhere on this Journey
You wiped away
my tears,
gave light to my
deepest fears,
reminded me that I
was more than my
past,
gave me inspiration
to make my dreams
last

Somewhere, if I never
get to say,
know I love you all
till the end of my days

Exacerbate

Becoming increasingly sharp, bitter, violent, challenging or unpleasant

Things happen in our lives. To keep it real, people happen in our lives. They speak, touch, walk, talk and push in ways which are challenging, unpleasant, bitter, violent, unsettling and life altering.

This trauma leaves lifelong scars. Our scars are visible and invisible. Looking at me, you would not know how racism, sexism, violence, being underpaid, rarely promoted, not heard, left behind, discounted and devalued has impacted the story of my life. People have no idea how their behavior changes another person's life. We don't see how trauma impacts their walk, their potential – every cell of their being.

But it is important to know that your actions, deeds, policies, beliefs, ignorance (known and unknown) and choices have consequences. I am my brother and my sister's keeper, and I must own my impact.

I smile everyday because I live in God's grace and mercy. I honor the next step of this journey, Exacerbate. I recognize these experiences came to teach, stretch and grow me.

I Am Here! Thriving! May these WORDS ground your faith, remind you that you are not alone, and breathe life into the endless possibilities of OUR collective futures.

Experience Exacerbate and may the WORDS dance from my Spirit and into your Soul!

YOU

You
have used me
Taken my private space
Entered me like a hunter
Stalking its victim's sacred place

You held me
You took and
Conquered

Against a wall
Against time
Destroying my self-respect
Condemning
My Mind

I
truly
want to hate
To dig down
into a pit of revenge
Where   evilness   manifests   itself
into
Aggression
Where you now lie
limp - nude
Where your self-respect
is characterized
By submission

No holy water
No sermon on the Hill
Nothing washes away the film
Except the destructive desire to kill

Who gave him the right
to
Condemn me
to life
Imprisonment
When You
Allow him
the Right
To Live

"On a street called Anna, in a city called Elizabeth,
there is a house that once housed red furniture
covered by plastic in a dark room. The room
was not only dark because it lacked light but because
the humans were lacking. Alcoholism, selfishness,
lack of accountability, disconnectedness and abuse held court
on a street called Anna in a city called Elizabeth.
At age seven and eight, for months, you took my innocence!
You distorted truth and the meaning of family, stole trust, and
threatened the life of my father all to keep me silent.
Your choices altered my life!
A flippant apology to our family is not an apology to me
for the crimes you committed.
My mouth is no longer bound.
Forgiveness is a journey and a choice. I chose faith, therapy
and self- healing. You are left to your demons...
those following you from the house on a
street called Anna - in a city called Elizabeth."

According to the Center for Violence Against Black Women,
1 in 4 black girls will be raped by the age of 18
and 1 in 5 black women are survivors of rape.

WHAT WOULD I TELL YOU

What
would I tell you
if you
were not
more religious
than faithful
You
who have mastered
chapter and verse
but
whose words
sting -
feel
less
like love,
more
like a curse
You
who live in judgment
Abusing the Word,
to rule and control
others,
no longer
can you engage me,
no longer hold you
in the "best" category
You
who speak about
being
outside a circle
must
question
your own heart

HOLD YOUR PEACE

The words and actions
roll
off your tongue,
form
from your fingers,
project
from your attitude,
flow
from your eyes

You
who love the Lord,
who quote
passage and verse
Speak to Me
and the language,
the body language,
feels more
like a
Curse

Hold
Your Peace
whispers my spirit
Hold
Your Peace
for this is not
your battle
Hold
Your Peace
This is but
A distraction

Then come the
fractions
Where your words
don't equal
the
equation
of your faith
Or
maybe it does
for certain people
in certain places of faith

For You
to call Me
Desperate
To be "okay"
with my less
Did nothing to
enhance your position
in my heart
Once a place of tenderness

What you are
Experiencing
Is not
the love and faith of 'ol
It's
Holding My Peace
Hoping God Saves My Soul

NOT AFRAID

You talk to me
but it is
not kind
not encouraging
not filled with joy
No love,
you seem to
want me
gone
You want me to
rid myself from
this planet
You
want my existence
to be a
memory

Before I deposit
my gifts
my talents
my purpose
you
dance in my head
with reminders of
my pain,
my past,
who hurt me,
who hurts me
I hear
the laughter
the defeat
the looks
I feel
the "less than"
existence
My eyes are open
But you

block me from seeing
my tomorrow
But today
I moved from
the side,
the back,
from disappointment
and lack
I moved
to a position
sitting on the
Master's lap
All my history and all
my ancestors
Sang Hallelujah,
Taking my Purpose
Back
I am no
longer Afraid
What is left to take
My things,
oh my mind
You had a grip on it
for a long time
I am
not Afraid
because
His words
ring true
He died for me
and for you
I am
not Afraid,
standing in mass or alone,
wearing my
helmet,
carrying the Holy Spirit
in me
I am at peace
I'm finally
Home

JUST THE LITTLE GIRL

I write to you
because I'm having a hard time
grasping your experience
I have left you for
non-existent
for so long
that
facing you is hard
Dealing with
what you went through
seems like counseling someone else
I celebrate your
survival
and
your arrival
to this day
But
Owning It,
Owning You
is hard
I feel so sad
and deeply hurt
by the
taking of your
Essence
and
Our private space
I see you
in my head
and it is all
Trauma
The who and the what
is Trauma
I don't want to
forsake you
But
I have lived

my life
with you
being
over there,
somewhere
Yet, as I walk
this second half of my life,
you have not
been
over there - somewhere
You have sat
in my choices
You have held
on to my pain
You have spoken
to my
memories
You have trickled
down my face,
tears and pain

You call to me
like a child lost
in the night
We are not
two separate people
It's I and WE
in this fight
I'm just the little girl
You are all grown up
But
What was done to me
Was done to you
God, make us both free
Not free
in your niceness
But
Free
In your anger and disbelief,
Free from the
bondage -
Emotional,

Mental,
Physical
Just Relief
You have to see Me,
Speak to Me in
the place
We call home
Sitting here in your heart,
Broken and alone
Please dial 911
Help needed
for all this filth
I suppressed
Here
in the present
You have to
come get me
The signs for
Rescue
are everywhere
'cause
Us
You
All of me
Was
the only One
Forced
to "lie"
Just the little Girl
speaking to the woman
Working
to heal
Our soul
from up out of trauma
We are Striving
As One
Together
We are Whole

AT THE END

What would you know
of my pain?

It sits in every cookie,
every pound I gain!

To pull out the glass,
pour one more
bottle to pass
my pain
Just goes down the drain
called my lungs

You don't see the scars
The words come via text,
sitting alone,
any place,
always waiting
for what's next

Pulling it together,
you think truth
will make me thin?

Just so very tired
Here's where that
overweight, alcoholic,
who's been abused
and
abused herself is at
the end

DON'T

Don't want to be
fake
in my feelings
Don't know how
to cry
without feeling
It's too much
gone on too long
Seeking sympathy
but in my most
still moments
or when I
move a certain way,
head in a certain direction
"YOU" come at me
with such force
of emotion
Don't know what to say
so I keep asking questions
Questions
unease my ability to
separate
from my feelings
my zillion stories

Who am I
hiding inside myself,
inside a dark room
with couch covers,
inside where the sweaty legs
stick to plastic
where my fake self
took over my real self

Not that
I don't have
a good heart,
that I don't love y'all
but it hurts to love
so I'm in
and I'm out
Want to be present
but I just am tired,
tired leads to
just don't care
but I care very much
Rising off that couch,
determining who I would
be
No one to tell the
shame of being me

Don't want to be
fake
Little girl inside
is due her Dew and her Dawning
resurrection of her
spirit
God's light to shine
through
Don't want to be fake
Tears seem like they're
a quadruple threat -
father, mother, little girl
and the grown women
I haven't met yet

But with these writings
she's coming

POWER

What does it mean
to have
power?
One single moment:
given
taken away
born with
born without
connected to privilege
disconnected from truth
inside
external
in and out of my title
in and out of my feminity
in and out of my color

Surrounded by people
who walk in privilege,
yield power
from the unconsciousness
of their existence
Is it fragility
or an inability to come
to grip with their
weakness,
false sense of creation

BREASTS

You see these
Breasts,
Full
and Ready
Stop pretending
your imagination
is not getting the best of you

You was talking
all sweet to me,
staring down at my
Breasts
instead of up at my face

I don't mind
we ain't gonna be together
for a long time
I'm not sensitive
about these things,
not trying to keep you,
don't want no
wedding ring

Just keep talking
to my breasts
with your feeble
little mind
'cause all this
intellectual capital
is navigating your ignorance,
one promotion
at a time

AUDACITY

You have no idea
what it's like to live
your life through
flashes of events,
then the brain
opens up and the flash
becomes lightning
which is the storm
before the tsunami
All of those who
took, against will,
by force
the essence of another's
freedom and another's
soul
The rest will never understand
how minor details matter
It is not just
my memory,
it's my pain

Pain from your
audacity to take
then show up
at my momma's wake
What a time to
make your presence
known,
The Audacity

Hidden Inside of Me

The good girl
wants to tell
all the reasons
you should be proud

The angry woman
wants to show
you
her hurt,
her stain,
all the reasons
she's so loud

The grieving daughter
wants you to remember
the commitments made
that changed her life

The divorced woman
wants you to know
how deep the wound
went
from the lies, cheating
that turned her world
upside down

The little girl
wants to be heard
for her voice has been drowned out
by a hand
of a man,
who cared little
and no doubt
took what
was not his
in a room
colored red,
leaving her with no perceived

power
and no voice

The woman
who had the courage
to sit in therapy
for the death of a parent
through the death of another,
fighting to come up and out
of the zillion bed spreads
and covers,
wants you to know
the journey and work
are as long and deep as the sea,
some parts exciting,
some plain scary

The woman who writes
and publishes her words
has opened up to be free,
so no longer my past
Hiding Inside of Me

To live in my falsehood
when it seemed not safe
feels like another woman
and sometimes one really
bad dream

The woman
who writes this
finds freedom at last
'cause she realizes
she's more than her past

It came to teach her
so she could write
once more
that all the
people she's been
have been the key
to her future
and so very much more!

TIME WAS NOT KIND

Time was not kind
to the skin
of the kinfolk
It ate away
at the heart of
their home,
too much fussin'
at the stuff
not done,
not much words
left,
no victories won

Time was not kind
to the mother
alone,
having had one child
whose footsteps
still roam
in the wrong
park,
just left her with
memories,
white chalk
outlined his
space

Time is not kind
to the man
tied to the back
of the truck,
dragged for hours,
worse than a dog,
pieces of life
left on the road

Time is not kind
to the country
in peril
Our treatment of
each other
ruthless and sterile
400years
and rights are
still wrong
Basic decency
is being searched out,
feels like so much
is gone

Time is not kind
for the truth it
will one day bear,
that you stole, lied
and decimated
for no reason at all
except to feed greed,
cover up your real fear

Tick Tock Tick Tock
Reality is here!

Did You

I wish we didn't
need
to hurt and destroy
other people
It is in our nature,
just like diseases
exist in our bodies

Those diseases don't always
manifest in ways we see
and this is what I
say for those
who came to hurt and destroy:
Somewhere,
somehow
your chromosomes crossed,
your education was misguided,
and master sold you
mis-education
Did you ever research
what you were fed?
Ever take the time to listen to any
of those questions in your head?

Is it easier to
hurt and destroy?
Did you learn from your religion that
what you do to others
returns to you and yours with a
vengeance?

Do you believe that just eliminating
people and truth will save you?
You must
because you continue
to let others dip you
into the bath of fear and
pretend
self preservation

The earth is dying
Man is not only killing it
but each other
What little thing
you feel
you can control
will amount to nothing
You will be left to rule
over dogs and pestilence,
man's two best friends
Choose your behavior
The world deserves better

FRAGILE

How fragile
might you be

The shakiness
of the water,
inconsistency of
your existence,
the false belief
that this is
our America
our history
our truth
So tired,
overwhelmed
some days by
the loss of
my daughters and
my sons
Loving God
but struggling to
love and to do
what He asked me
To love my neighbor
as myself

How do I do
what your fragility
keeps you
from doing?
You who love Jesus
You who speak to democracy
You who judge
with no knowledge
no courage
no capacity
You who hold court
arms crossed, hate symbols
no truth in your hands

The scales of justice
broke
a long time
ago,
not sure
it
ever existed
Weighted down
by lies
by fear
by fragility
Blind,
willfully so
Truth is
powerful
Call it unconscious
if you choose
more of an
excuse
to those
who
lose

How fragile might you be?

CAN'T BREATHE

Can't breathe,
the truth
is suffocating

The room
surrounds me,
bombards me
with sound

The noise
bounces off
the wall

The words
where you
hurt them,
where you took
and never gave,
where you study
as bodies
after bodies
go to unmarked
graves

How many years did
you study
the Native Americans,
the Japanese,
why can't we
breathe

Because it is all
just noise,
never real
intent to
address 400
years of
evil and destruction

BROTHERS AND SISTERS SHOUT

Oh my sisters
how I sometimes forget
that there is so much more that
lies beyond your African beauty
I sometimes forget
that when I was weak
or when I was denied my rights
you stepped in and stepped up
to the fight

Yes, I get disappointed
when you find only the negative
in me
your Black man
When you let society dictate
your reaction to me and
your interaction with me
But mostly when
you lose faith in me and
lump me into a predisposed
TV- and magazine-created image
that says I'm doing drugs, beating my kids
turned gay or living in jail
All of us are not in those categories
We are trying to help
carry the load
We are seeking peace with you,
my sister,
and in that peace
we will discover love, understanding, respect
and the birth of a stronger Black union
For you see, my beautiful sister,
We, your brothers, will follow you
Anywhere
thus
It is time to let the truths out

demanding each other's respect
this I pledge to you
Black Brothers Shout!

My Brothers,
from the day they put chains
around your feet and hands
I - We,
your sisters,
have prayed for you
We prayed that the essence
of your African soul
manhood
Would not be locked in
chains too
Yet, society has another chain
for you to release
yourself from
and
they bear both our names

I sometimes forget
that my success
is our success
as a race
and for every step
forward for me
Your steps may not be
as large
or steps at all
Our society
loves and hates me
as much as you
and
with the same lack of understanding
I pray
that you always take the
strength of
the next African Kings
to push forward
and realize

Queens
have led the battles won also

As a team,
We will find our place
on the throne
As a team,
We will give birth to a nation of children
Who love themselves
because they know
their contributions to a country
that does not always
recognize them
It is not enough to know
American History
We must know
African History
Our love making
is and
must be
Strong
and
intense
Two minds and souls
creating a force
that clears
created underlying meanings and doubts
Oh, my Black Brother
I believe in you
All of you
I shall always stand behind you
this I pledge to You
Black Sisters Shout!

WHEN SISTAS GET
TIRED

See, when sistas get tired,
when they get angry
and blue,
it is usually perceived to be about a
relationship
but it's really with the system
They tired
of getting screwed

It's too much pressure,
like living two lives
It's about the inner turmoil,
which way does one strive

Folks like to tell
women they are all the same
but there are unique differences,
"two-fer" is not what we claim

Don't possess the status
to sit on center court
nor drink through college,
making marriage
my sport

Don't have the money
to buy status or fame,
just my God-given talents,
my strength and my determination
to claim

See, when a sista
gets tired,
her head hangs low,
her senses dull
and her spirit,
it's aura, don't glow
She is always on guard,
feeling persecuted and shamed,
planning to run toward peace,
hoping to hit the Big Lotto game

Yet, at the end of that journey
when rest comes
and fears relieved,
a sista
regains that energy,
that spark,
her power
See,
that's what sistas do
'cause
sistas will
achieve

Angry Day in the Life

You would think
that after all that has been done,
we would not have to walk this route
again and again and again

Your ability to drop seeds of evil
never ceases to amaze me
If it were not for the faith I possess
and my ability to recognize
through every experience comes
learning,
I would throw my hands up and scream

I would enter my floor
and hold an "automatic" over their head,
no intent to harm
but asking for the TRUTH

Why do you needle my folks,
spend your lifetime poking and prodding
You can't add up the damage done
from your stares, words, images, actions,
your deliberate silence,
your private clubs,
your meetings in the men's room
The way you cluster together
to convene upon the
only soul who looks
nothing like
you

THE COVERING

We are human
We are strong,
vulnerable
to truth -
right or wrong
Hustling,
Shuffling
Muscling our way
Not totally
Conscious
of what
impacts
other humans' day
Full of opinion
shaped by faith, fact, fiction and fear
Not always exact
on how we "got here"
Governing, smothering, stuttering
this dance
History asking
did we all have a chance
So here in this moment,
offer
a different world view
Moving out of coloring, numbering and puncturing,
getting a clue
For it is time to
start shoveling, ushering, restructuring,
uncovering these tasks
to bring an end
to the silent suffering
where we all
wear our
Masks

TRANSITION

You ever
sit at work
and wonder
WTF am I
doing here?

People are talking,
not making sense,
or they make sense
but no one is going to
support their
brilliance
Do these
people
have a clue
what you do?

Does anyone remember
the basics?
Ask us a question
before functioning
in your
big
idea,
might your
big idea
be old crap
with some pretty
multi-colored sprinkles
to trick listeners
into becoming participants

We just recycle
ideas
ourselves
each other
until
there is no more
rinse and repeat
cycle
left for us to hit

Then we sit still
and ask
WTF
am I doing here?

Ventilator

How
in the silence
does a heart
make peace
with a hand
they will never
touch
again
a heart
whose beat
has met
quiet and stillness
alone
How
when they were
just
holding their children
celebrating special occasions
providing for their families
driving a bus
in a CARE facility
going to work or church
How
do we say
goodbye
When It Feels Like...
We've been
robbed
hoodwinked
bamboozled
by both a
disease and a
dis-ease
in the land
We have lost
too many souls

I struggle to
see if I still
can
move forward
Believe
in the greater good
this virus
ravishing homes, communities
my neighborhood
Calling on
the hearts of
science and the faith based
Calling on the ONE
Alpha and Omega
who beckons us to question our comfort
who reminds us that
no one gets out alive
We share
this 1st Heaven
it is never too late
to cure the disease killing mankind
Before, during and after the arrival of COVID-19
The Earth is breathing
Light has given way to the depth of hunger, poverty, violence, disparity,
injustice, ignorance,
Selfishness and in some spaces evil
We miss the connection...
not knowing, not wanting to know, not asking, not caring...
as people... as humans... as leaders
if enough ventilators and PPEs exist
if the lives of those on ALL the front lines are not
worthy enough to stand your ground
and stay at home
to be blessed to still have the opportunity to
be with those in your life who are
still living
This disease before, during and "after" COVID-19 is the real killer
rotting in the core of our souls
fear, greed and selfishness holding humanity hostage
rushing to get back to "power"
for a people who have never been controlled

Again, it is the same as
not knowing, not wanting to know, not asking and not caring
about 41 million starving Americans yet our farms had food go to waste
in this pandemic
the need to make a video to address the acts of discrimination and racism
placed upon Asian people
Why are All these acts so easily done?
'Cause the disease arrived long ago…
We are not students of truth and research
but many are privileged hosts of consequences
because in the 1800s that same discrimination and racism
pained Irish immigrants to the US with employment signs that read,
"No Irish Need Apply"
pained Italian immigrants where papers alleged,
"Mediterranian types were greatly inferior to the Northern Europeans"
and the KKK lynched Italians,
pained the Jews in Nazi death camps,
pained the Japanese in US internment camps,
pained India under British rule,
pained the forced relocation of 60,000 Native Americans
during the Trail of Tears where over 4,000 died,
pained black and brown people across the globe
in places like Asia and Australia where their land was stolen
and where their skin relegates them to
"not existing and not being part of the culture,"
pained Muslims, Sikhs, and persons of Arab and South-Asian descent
after 9/11,
pained children in 2019 locked in cages and separated from their families,
pain and residue experienced by the enslaved and the descendents of the
enslaved 400 years and counting…
pained by another list of black and brown senseless deaths
we can't breathe from the noose, to illegal chokeholds, to breaking in at
wrong addresses, to 41 bullets, to taking a knee
Not free… not safe from the disease of COVID-19
nor racism circa 1600 to 2021
there are no free passes
History has called us to pause
'Cause what you want for "you" is

Required for ALL
Our country's mere existence is on a ventilator
COVID-19, killer hornets, murdering of innocence
are on a long list of signs
"A Change Gonna Come"
People, you, we, me are being challenged to
Own and accept a new fabric must be spun
if a more truthful and just Union is to survive
the boomerang tossed out to harm others
has come
again and again and again and again
there are no free passes - comes for us all
Our beloved country is a serious case of this disease
Damage to our lungs and body
Oxygen levels dropping lower for centuries
Making it harder for people to breathe
To find and live in America's call for democracy
Ventilators push air
With increased levels of oxygen
It's the humidifier
Which adds heat and moisture to the air supply (research and truth)
Matches the patient's body temperature (goal of one America)
Sometimes, patients need medication to relax
(stay at home - wear your mask - protect others - respect those on the
front lines)
These desperate acts to breathe
Each of us, free, own our own, together and safe
Are our increased levels of oxygen
this global air the virus helped clear
against centuries of fear, doubt, selfishness, inequity, injustice and history
shaping lies
Centuries of wanting "just for me and mine"
Keeping us all poor, literally and figuratively
Paining others and other kinds
Of not knowing, not wanting to know, not asking and not caring
America, see who truly stands for
Your written values
You'll find those people by the ventilators
Finally, sharing...

Ezekiel 37:4-14

Again He said to me, "Prophesy over these bones and say to them, 'O dry bones, hear the word of the Lord.' Thus says the Lord God to these bones, 'Behold, I will cause breath to enter you that you may come to life. I will put sinews on you, make flesh grow back on you, cover you with skin and put breath in you that you may come alive; and you will know that I am the Lord."

Spirituality

Affecting the human spirit or soul; sacred; divine; secular and nonsecular; churchly and holy

For me, FAITH is the hallmark of my journey. My soul has traveled the path set forth for it, and there are days of great joy and days of sorrow. When I look back over my life, through the lens of my poetry, I was raised to believe in God and in the hope of the resurrection. I don't shy away from my beliefs and I respect the beliefs of others.

Believers, no matter what their faith, may struggle. I believe we are all spiritual beings having a human experience. It's painful losing who and what we love. It's hard walking through the world when it sometimes feels absent of the empathy and compassion we desire. Over the journey, it was challenging when my path wasn't clear and the waiting seemed like a lifetime.

I must own my choices because there are no TRUIMPHS without tribulations... without stretching. When it seemed like there was no way, when counted down and out, when questions and doubts lingered, when challenges kept surmounting, loving family, friends, church sermons, kind words, helpful hands, therapy, hugs, love, laughter and my faith lifted my spirits and kept me strong.

Experience a Spiritual triumph and may the WORDS dance from my Spirit and into your Soul!

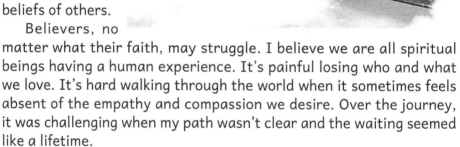

ASKING TO GO

When grief introduced itself to you,
you did not realize it

I understood
Grief was taking your breath away

You were not able to see how
Grief met me
It walked into the boxing ring
called life
and it played with me
round after round
Even when the bell sounded
there was no rest
from grief
It punched my head and heart
"Down goes Frazier"
"Down goes Harris"

Grief stood around me
and over me
like Foreman did Frazier
It knew I would not
step away from my calling

It knew You
were never fully going to heal
It felt both the anger of loss
and the question of freedom,
and I knew
nothing would ever be the same

All I wanted to do
was sit by myself
in my own sadness
to feel my own tears,
collapse in my own weakness,
decide not to move on
But I was destined
to be present,
destined to watch

the ever changing landscape
of your pain,
your multi-level loss
and disappointment

Maybe
you were afraid
and as much as I believed
I could help,
I could not calm your fears,
had no ability to
completely
wipe away your tears
They began
before I entered the world

I would stand over you
at night,
praying
for your pain,
the trauma in your life
before and during the time
I entered the world

In his absence,
I wanted you
to choose me,
choose life
The limb was taken
Another question to God
about why "so much pain"
Why, God, is there so much pain in the world?
Bounced back physically
but the mind and spirit
"down like Frazier"

So Asking to Go
seemed cruel to me
What was so wrong that you could not stay
with me?
Somehow and someway

I was not enough
"Down goes Harris"

Asking to Go felt selfish and cruel
because
I
had happy dreams
of the life
filled with love and joy
Maybe
'cause
I never
"Asked to Go"

I ran to you
You said, "You're going to miss me when I'm gone"
I was missing you while you were present
Hurt and trauma
Strips us
Not enough to go to church,
Gotta open up and let your faith
Heal you

I miss both of you

Not a day in my life
I don't recognize my triangle
is now a straight line

Grateful God planted me in
your life,
for your absence has been a journey
transitioning from Frazier
to Foreman
Understanding that
"Asking to Go"
was your antidote
to the number of boxing rounds,
never the answer to my worth

Just the need
we all have
to live free

ONCE FEAR MET ME

Once fear met me,
it loved me,
it danced around me,
celebrated me
It was the focus
of my gifting

Once the music
fear created
changed,
my world was rearranged,
so much taken
from my life,
heart was broken,
fear created strife

But today
I live like this no more,
put up my fist,
kicked down hell's door

Once it laughed
and called me
it's b—
Drowning my words
and future
into its darkest pit,
Thinking less of me
with its blanket
spread wide
smiling nicely
'cause I
abide

Fear it said
held me close,
grasping my throat,
finding its ego to boast

But like Ali
it heard my mighty voice
This battle's over,
you have no choice
Down goes fear
Down you go

Victory
Salvation
Publication
Movie Nation
HBCU Sensation

My gifting through God
has been
Consecrated

REST ASSURED

Where does the child go
when the adult is expected
to live and behave
according to the rules

What does the child,
the one living inside of the adult, do
when the adult self
wants to drop to the
floor,
throw a tantrum,
kick and scream,
and speak ill
to the "thing" that
brought them to that day
Rest Assured
there are no easy feelings,
no one really
believing that
my behavior is normal,
correct or true
I just ain't sure
I got nothing left
My inner child
can't be controlled
and
Rest Assured
the adult me is
through
What am I left with
under all these tears,
covered by all this anger
Rest Assured
is the feeling of absence
speaking to my heavenly father,
speaking to my faith
Where are you?

To My Lord

To my Lord,
to my bestie,
my daddy,
counselor,
friend:
Thank you
over and over again

For all things
big and small
For relationships
that surpass
them all
For connections
which bridge the gap
For the lessons learned,
stuff I can't take
back
For parents
you freely gave,
then set free
the heartbreak
that sits beneath me

Thank you
for words
to help me write
Thank you for
good mornings
after good nights

Peace
Time
Sitting still
alone in my mind
Grace hovers about me
Through the dew and
the sunshine

I Walk In Grace

I walk in Grace
I walk in the thrill
of what you will do
for the world

I walk in Grace
Grateful to be doing
what you asked
when you asked
Grateful to be present

My morning dew
lingers over my spirit
The joy is lasting
to the core of my being

I walk in Grace
Mercy has found me too
What else could I do
but be grateful
everyday
for your love

TALKING IT OVER

Talking it Over
with God
being present in
the moment
because of His Grace

Talking it Over
with God
the One who
gave me
Power

The God
who sees all
The God
that pushes us
to places and spaces
hidden beyond
ourselves

Hidden but
ever present
to our souls

Talking it over
with God
His Grace
His Mercy
is
Real

CELEBRATING POSSIBILITIES

What if God
answered prayers
What if You
received what you
prayed about
prayed for
How would you
invite it in
care for it
fight for it
feed it
grow it
love it
What if the answers
to the prayers
lived inside
You
What if God
answered your prayers
Did you
care for it
fight for it
feed it
grow it
invite it in
Did You
love you?

WHEN IN DOUBT

When in doubt
come to me
Come to me
on your knees
in prayer
in expectation
in trouble
in question

Let go of false
pretenses
that give you
expectations
of freedom

Questions
are better
than
assumptions

When In Doubt
Come

COMING FOR YOU

He's coming for me
He's placed all His attention
on ensuring
I live out my
purposed driven life
He's calling me now
in ways
I understand
and question

He's coming for me
to ensure
the light of my gifts
are given away
to His Glory
These gifts don't
blow
like leaves
across the vast land
and concrete
belonging to nothing
and no one,
seeds displaced,
roots withered,
completely fallen
This is why

He's coming for me
in my head,
through my heart,
engulfing my body
dancing in my soul
You will see the
manifestation of Him

Just Wait

Just Wait on the Lord
For He will grant you the love of your life
He will send your soulmate,
Wrapped in truth,
Focused on faith,
Dipped in endless possibilities
The Lord will wipe loneliness and fear from your heart

Just Wait

When seconds tick and days go by
Just wait
When the sheets are cold
Just wait
When tear-stained pillows don't support you
Just wait
When Edward, William, Tyson, George, Kevin, Al, Dave and Pookie
Wish to know you only in the
midnight hour
Just wait
When Tamisha, Karen, Susan, Sharon, Kineka, Andrea, Denise and Robin
Wish to know your income, the vehicle you drive,
your zip code and your PIN number

Just Wait

Never settle for less than your dreams
Never expect or ask for more than you are willing to do
Never aspire to be less than God created
Never covet your neighbor's "goods"

See, the goods you covet
Will fall short of your expectations once
the temptation has been realized

You, my dear sisters,
will wreak havoc
on the life of another sister
In the name of the pillow
once

clenched between your legs
You will justify your actions and
point to her shortcomings
Just so you don't have to
accept your role in her pain
As if you don't remember
or can't relate to her pain
If he was pre-determined
to be your "pillow,"

It would not be at the expense of
another sister's tears

Just Wait

You, my dear brothers,
will produce havoc on your offspring
In the name of body parts for
which most of you have described as

"seen one, seen them all"
This statement must fall short of the truth because
the resistance to "same" seems to apply only
To the woman who waits on you and for you at home
It does not seem to cross your mind
that sons are born and
nurtured to be like you
everyday

In fact, your behavior
guarantees that
your offspring - female child
will ensure her painstaking place
on the throne of heartbreak
For as the movie said, "if you build it, they will come"
Instead of building a testimony
to the love of God
through
a solid relationship,
You build a legacy of
mistrust and tears

Just Wait

Do not let age dictate your soulmate
Do not let loneliness, debt, greed, selfishness, ego, status, appearance,
body shape, height and weight
Dictate your soulmate

Just Wait
Just Wait!

YOU COULD NEVER

You would never believe the power
the gift of words and the
twisting of them holds

You would never understand
the loneliness
and the total wholeness which comes

Not from myself but
from God
who loves me
more than I could love myself
or hope to love those around me

You would never believe the power
and sheer terror responsibility brings
when talent runs wild
and fear is neck and neck

You could never touch the force
of the spirit
which lies within me,
fighting me
for me
A battle which hopes for sweet victory

You could not begin
where the story ends
For your start is my middle
and for every life there is
a middle

You could never
'cause never
is a word
you should not
subscribe to

HOLD COURT

Make time for Me
Hold court on your
knees
to pray
Give me what is due
as I bless you
everyday
Never a reason
to doubt me
Yet, I know
in your humanity
it's hard sometimes
to count on Me
But I bring you
through
every time
It may not be
what you expect
Sometimes
abundance
comes
in very different ways
You
are always
walking in favor,
my beautiful and gifted children,
even
when you disobey
For my love
knows no boundaries
No secrets between
you and I
I sent my Son
to the cross
to redeem you
to Eternity
He spread his arms

and hung high
But on that
faithful day,
He rose again,
redeeming all
your sins
Justifying hands
clasped
and
knees bent
For I love you
now and always,
to death
we never part
'Cause I am
your Creator,
the reason
for your
beating heart
Make time for Me
Hold court on
your knees
and pray
For I am
the
Alpha and Omega,
bright morning star
The Word is my
direction,
guiding you
all the way

DRY HANDS

Here I sit Lord
Move me out of the way
Make my limited human knowledge
Still
Maybe my pixie dust
Was truly my survival tool
My hands are dry
My nails are breaking
I'm listening to everyone
Who can motivate me
But this dryness is not shaking
You are teaching me something
While my hot flashes are raging
Feels like its own form of darkness
Trying to fight to keep changing
Darkness

The lotion is useless
Dry lines come back every day
Cuticles are dry
White
Damaged
Me
Doesn't matter how much lotion
Dryness
Seeps through

Here I sit Lord
Your saved and redeemed
Covered by the blood
Saved by grace
But in need of
Mercy
Dryness is a thorn
Believing
Can make you worn
From age 8 to today
Emotionally torn
Where is my lotion
Where are the emollients

Created for those who
Have been told to
"F" themselves
Staying "focused" on my
Future blessings
Takes some of the itch away
Ain't my dryness
In my head
Heart
Spirit
Health
And pocket
Aren't I like Jobe
Dryness coming
Everyday

Baptize me
Again
Maybe the water will
Wash away the pain
Maybe it will
Not dry me
Maybe the Word
Will make me whole again
Cause this lotion
Is useless!

"L"

As the days pass,
your absence still causes me to cry
I've been to the cemetery
I vow not to return
It is too hard

To bury one parent
took my breath away
To stand
on the grass
where both of you
lay beneath my feet
causes my heart to ache,
tears to continuously flow
And the struggle between
gratefulness for your peace
and no pain
conflicts with sadness for my loss,
tearing at my spirit,
straining
acceptance
that three is now
one
Of the three Christmas stockings
with our initials,
only "L" remains

In our case
the "L"
will represent love
Love brought us together
Love will hold us
Absent the physical contact,
love will hold us,
absent the sound of your voices,
absent the touch

The "L"
will represent lasting
Our family,
our love for each other
is and will always be
lasting

Sovereignty

Jurisdiction; dominion; independence; control; authority; determination; freedom; influence

So much of Sovereignty is about the right to dance free in the mind and skin I am in. I have always had thick thighs and sometimes carried extra pounds. My dad said I should have been a runner instead of a ballerina. Those thick thighs were the reason my dance instructor would not let me progress to toe shoes. I was surrounded by tall, thin and beautifully gifted dancers. Every time the instructor told me, "no," and those girls laughed, I worked harder. The day arrived when those pink toe shoes were mine, illuminating early steps on the path of determination and freedom.

There are places and spaces I was not expected to be or inhabit, but the music of my life kept me dancing. My dreams kept me believing in the potential to be great.

I struggled with boundaries, people pleasing and seeking approval. The desire to be a "good girl" did not always create safety nor the results I expected.

These experiences are gifts: growth, independence and the courage to continue stretching. I am so grateful to raise my eyes and hands to the heavens, knowing what an amazing journey has transpired!

Like Dorothy in *The Wiz,* I click my heels, believing my WORDS are my "no place like home."

Experience Sovereignty's dance and may the WORDS dance from my Spirit and into your Soul!

DECIDE

I feel you
a million miles away
The room is smokey,
filled with people
waiting for you to
bring on the joy

Hoping that words
move them,
DJ finds the rhythm
to soothe them

To give peace to
the crazy,
a week where common sense
left the building,
common sense was tired of
pretending

I feel your
practice
Don't matter how many times
the words have
rolled off your tongue,
taught it's day one
all
over
again

So feel the
encouragement
Be the gift you are
intended to be
Give them a new level
Make 'em laugh to the end
Placing your future
in God's grace,
doing it
consistently
over and over again
I want to

DECIDE
not that I'm
worthy
but that
absent my
presence,
this will not be
a place
of
peace
Come on,
Decide!

VERSION II

She
is a disruptive,
pulling together
light and dark,
giving out
fire,
eruption,
spark,
twist and turns
Direction not clear
to the naked eye
but
disruptors
know,
never disconnected
from her purpose,
fire giving birth to more flames

She came to
make a difference
You don't need
to know
her name
She
is the she
of purpose
not fame

YOU WILL RELEASE

You will let me out
You will remember
this gut that
opened up from
the blow of
sorrow and sadness

You will set me free,
free from the madness,
free to laugh,
free to run and dance
naked
in the essence of me,
this body,
this time

You will know my purpose
not because you
own it or
control it
but because it's
coming to release
the captives,
to provide mental
and emotional
release

You will Release Us
for your time is up
You will stop hiding
behind ignorance
which is actually
privilege,
stop pretending you don't
see it,
benefit from it,
make money off of it

You will end your
righteous indignation
in one space of your
life
yet
live blind in other
spaces
To not see is choice,
to not change is choice,
to continue your privilege
is grounded
in fear
It is criminal

You will release yourself
Only this will change
the world
so we all can run naked
and dance in truth

WALKING UPRIGHT

Walking upright
Ain't it a joy
to be fully engaged
in life,
finally feeling like
fun with my toys
Got the land
Got the stage
Got the money
Got the play
Got the love of my life
to dance me
through life
So easy to be me
So wonderful to be granted
every life opportunity
to love, be true,
be mean or be blue
Just gotta stay
upright
not
uptight
'cause I gotta
get from where you
are
to who I
need to
be

IN

So many times
you come to us
in pain
in hurt
in abuse
to become the
abuser
So many people,
so much hurt,
too many children
left to divert
the acts
which rob their
personhood
In pain
in hurt
in abuse
becomes drugs
becomes alcohol
becomes sex
becomes food
Pay attention,
ask questions,
don't leave your child
alone
without tools or defense
Give them the freedom to tell you
they been touched
not by an angel
but by evil's pants or skirts
For silence, fear and pain
creates its own disdain
requiring years and years
of help
Give them a safe place to
break the gag

that binds their voice,
to purify the whole,
giving
the child
or now an adult
a freeing gift
to finally be
in
control

Dedicated to the millions of people who have been molested, raped, and abused. Written after watching Jessica Simpson speak about being abused and taking back her power and narrative for her life.

AS I DO THEM

How awesome my journey,
how long the ride
to victory
seems to my soul
Keep reaching towards
something
that will finally
make the journey
complete,
make it right
for my soul to finally
accept its
resting place

So very tired
of clichés
"Close but no cigar"
"Almost had it all"
When I have been
blessed
to deliver to this
planet so much more
than it feels
I
am giving
Tired
Tired
Tired

Want love
Want laughter
Want friendship
which leads to all of those
Maybe I am just
destined
to be with me
Tired Lord,

Tired
Tears fill my eyes
as I type
Many, many lonely
Saturday – Saturday nights

So really,
who cares about my tears,
who cares that I lost 34 pounds,
that I walked into a lion's den
and arrived on the other side
strong
Who cares that I walk into
the lion's den everyday,
in a work environment
where my race, my intellect and my gender
are constantly and forever
under fire,
under doubt
To exist in an environment
where some respect you and care
and some
with Christian Bibles on Sunday
malign and defame you
on Monday
Hurts my spirit
I take comfort in those
who treat me with respect
As I do them

UPON THE SHORE

Upon the shore
Where love is more
Than just the passing of
Emotional words

Love
Two individuals
Interconnected
By deeper values,
Personal acceptance,
Challenges in the future
And faith
The foundation of truth and
Longevity
Rings
Symbolizing eternity
Symbolizing commitment
Symbolizing strength
Symbolizing the unity of two SOULS
Upon the shore
Where
Passion
Romance
Laughter
Respect
Friendship
and
Endurance
Rest safely
May your todays
Be full of potential

And
Your tomorrows
Full of
Joy

I Wrote This Yesterday

I wrote this yesterday
Feeling like the evening stars
Were waiting on the answers
To questions
I had not asked myself

The type of questions
Which make us uneasy,
Uncomfortable, unready to
Hear the
Truth

I wrote this yesterday
Hoping that by today
You
Would have appeared
In some Knight uniform
Waiting patiently to save me
From the things I seem so unable
To rescue myself from

But like me
You arrive in a Don Quixote uniform
Rescuing the dream
But not the dreamer

The dreamer
Calling to the Heavens
Thinking
God
May not be listening
Not recognizing that time is defined
Very differently in His eyes

The dreamer
Ever faithful to the cause
Believing the plan created has purpose
Knowing that God created the dreamer

To achieve their life's mission
To achieve the dream

I wrote this yesterday
Knowing the dreamer
Did not walk close enough to the edge
Managing easily what can be controlled
Walking on egg shells for that which can NOT

I wrote this yesterday
Knowing the dreamer saw the same
Stars
Knowing that God is working on 'em
As God is working on me
Knowing the dreamer
Dreams of the same
Passion
Purpose
Faith
Revolution for change
Vision of uniting people
God's people

I wrote this yesterday
Looking at stars
And crying tears of
Expectation
Closing my eyes
And wanting more
More of what makes
You a man
Me a woman

More of what makes
Combined respect
A strong foundation
Combined dreams
Powerful
Combined passion
Everlasting
Combined purpose

Dedicated
Combined faith
Able to move MOUNTAINS

I wrote this yesterday
Believing that
I can rescue the dream
And the dreamer

I wrote this yesterday
Looking at the stars
Believing
God
Has made us
To be two
Powerful forces
When molded
As one
According to His word
Will make dreams
Destiny
Thus changing
The lives
Of EVERYONE!

I wrote this yesterday
With the sword
By my side
Watching you become KING
Ready as QUEEN

I'll be there
Looking up at the stars

QUOTES OF SOVEREGINGTY

WINGS OF LOVE
I once relished your wings of love until
Forced to Fly Solo
I discovered I had Wings of my Own

FRAGILE
Some time ago
you could never have told me
that what was once so fragile
is now at "normal" strength

PRIZE

Have I been dancing,
learning new steps
as the band changes beat?
Yeah, I've been dancing
My heart feels
the fire
put to my feet
Nothing like dancing
Life and dancing,
just the same
Both required
MOVEMENT
and a prolonged experience
could drive you,
leave you,
ake you
insane
But you better keep the pace
for losers never realize
just how close the race
Your distance is with destiny
A happy life is the
prize

EQUAL JUSTICE INITIATIVE – BRYAN STEVENSON

Often
Words of the Righteous
outweigh the truth
of Black and Brown people
seeking justice
in an
Unjust world

Rarely are words
so beautifully
hung together
than
when they
melodically
jump off the pages
of a brief
to cry out for
freedom,
to question
justice,
to call our moral
character
and our
God toting
verbatim of scripture
into question
while standing at
the hanging of
a human

There has never been justice,
"Just Us"
and you, Mr. Stevenson,
centuries of asking
"good people" to stand in the gap
for just us
for the gap is long,
wide and deep

It's still creepy,
asking "good people"
with the power to change
to take longer looks
in the mirror
The reflection is stained
with blood
How much more does
your hate
wish to take,
is our Jesus the same?

Mine came to set the captives free
Yours created an entire criminal industry
which exists from "sea to shining sea"

Use to think we could save 'em
from jail sentences longer
than a person's life span
Now got to keep them
from going into the system
working to make slaves out of
the black woman and man

Need more "good people"
who pick more than just one cause,
believe in all of them
Shouldn't a human life and its rights
give you greater pause

So blessings to the
warriors
who stand in and fight for
all genders and hues
for making this personal,
for it is similar to
the atrocities
experienced during the Holocaust

We have the opportunity to end
prison business - modern day extermination camps
But we must all believe
this is mass inhalation

As simple as it seems
because people are dying
There goes another loss
of our brothers and sisters...
"I Have A Dream"

Loving with Grace – Serving with Grit (Delta Sigma Theta Sorority, Inc.)

By definition,
being a Delta
is a woman of
grace
whose blessings
allow her to enter
places and spaces
to change,
to disrupt,
to move mountains
through her passion,
purpose and love
The Soul
of a Delta "Girl"
is sweet,
we know
Put a microscope
to the
Rich Redness of her
DNA -
Dedication, Navigation and Achievement
You
will experience
her G.R.I.T.
Delta Women
Generating Resources through Intelligence and Tenacity
Fueling futures,
executing strategies
strengthens
The Power of Our Sisterhood
from which
WE
deeply commit
from the heart
of a Delta
Loving with Grace and Serving with Grit

I KNEW I WAS DIFFERENT

I saw this picture
that's "me,"
next to the tall girl on your right,
not feeling "it,"
that promise
being realized from the marches for freedom and
Civil Rights
Even at that age,
I was different
I looked out to my future
I wanted the eyes of an eagle
to see far above this "land,"
the land I was asked to pledge allegiance to,
the one I was asked to love
Why would I love her?
America?
When she
has never shown love
to me and mine,
the dark and darker skin kind
Why would I
be excited about Freedom and Civil Rights?
Segregation and integration brought us the same outcome,
the facade of Freedom
When we was segregated,
we had communities like
Tulsa's Black Wall Street,
Rosewood
and more
Integration gave us
polite-whiteness,
people doing their "duty,"
still believing they better
Auctioning
their Sunday faith
I would say...

I'm a child - hopeful
but I see truth
I would look up past
the mouths of racism, sexism and evil
Looking up
gave me the sky
Looking out
helped me question
educated and documented lies
YOU wanted me to learn
your white-polite truth
where everyone in your history books
invented, created, developed and conquered
EVERYONE and EVERYTHING
I look at my picture
I knew I was different
I didn't believe you
It wasn't history that caused me to question your sincerity
It was your consistency that confirmed your moral character
Here I am in my late 70s
I still see the truth,
still looking up
Over the years
hope has been more of a question than a probability
Less years ahead of me and
I am
still questioning my Civil Rights,
still questioning true Freedom
Being free from the weight of
oppression,
micro and macro-aggressions,
conscious and unconscious bias,
hate and educated prejudice,
the continuation and justification of killing of our
daddies, mommas,
sisters, brothers,
neighbors, friends,
family and our children
Killed our past
Kill our present
Keep killing our future

America's
400-plus-year red claim ticket on
lives,
inventions,
creations,
developments and
accomplishments that were never yours,
Never... hers
I recall
during Pope John Paul II's 32 years
as the leader of the Catholic Church,
he apologized for the church's role
in every injustice against humanity
from Constantinople, Galileo, women, and
involvement in the slave trade,
inactivity and silence during the Holocaust,
violating rights of ethnic groups across the globe,
not supporting Rwandans,
and for not stopping Catholic priests from raping altar boys
I knew
the place that asked for my allegiance as a child,
America,
would not apologize
It would continue to immure dark and darker skinned people
I knew
as a child
that apologies without enforced policies
JUSTICE, EQUITY, EDUCATION and TRUTH
mean little to nothing to those
gasping for air,
to those whose hands are up and they can't breath,
and where you can't stand your ground
when the ground has never been there to support you
Even at that age,
I was different
Unfortunately,
60-plus years later
America
and the world
are still the same

Ecstasy

Joy; overwhelming emotion; swoon; excitement; prophetic trance and rapturous delight

How does one flow through feelings of ecstasy? Overwhelmed by passion, lust, excitement, and the possibility of entering a prophetic trance, we consciously step into rapturous delight. Oh, to have both our expectations and desires meet and sustain us. Where the connection to another gives birth to the curve of my hips and kisses on the lips. It's an inviting look, warm embrace, holding of hands or clasping them to pray which awakened the broken heart of a woman.

Ecstasy is emotional, mental and physical. It's imagination, connection and transformation grounded in truth and trust.

This collection of poems is about interrelatedness. It includes hope, quiet fantasies, explosions of desire and the joy and pain experienced from relationships. Many of us look and pray for love, craving a deeper connection to nourish the mind, body and soul.

In this season of my life, I seek God on the whereabouts of my true love, a man wise like King Solomon with the character of Boaz – neither perfect yet visionary and striving to walk in their purpose.

Through loving our Creator, we can learn to love ourselves and others – fully. Deciding to commit to a love greater than self, to sacrifice for the benefit of the whole, and to embrace the fire of our desire, is pure Ecstasy!

Experience the depth of mind and body that when intertwined births Ecstasy and may the Words dance from my Spirit and into your Soul!

HEY BEAUTIFUL

Hey Beautiful
Oops
You're handsome
Whatever
the words,
your presence is
stirring my
insides,
your memory
is calling to a moment
in time
when you,
when we
laid
legs intertwined
You
sunk in my divine,
neither moving,
neither seeming to care
We lay together,
daring
anyone or anything to
disturb
this presence,
this
rhythmic movement,
pulsating
sensations
Your presence is
stirring my insides,
Loving memories
Hey beautiful
Hey handsome
when
You coming home?

FORSAKEN

In this moment
when words have not
been shared,
when my legs wrapped around yours
given the impression
you cared
But silence
is a dangerous master,
leaves too much to the
imagination
Given all my hopes,
this feels like being
forsaken
Am I mistaken?
Feelings are
renewed,
intimidation and questions
are easily
misconstrued
Maybe
there are games to be played,
my confidence
to be shaken
Is this what it's like being
forsaken?

CAN I WANT YOU

Can I want you
and hold on to my
faith
Can I fantasize about
what might have been
if I had
more confidence,
more courage,
more belief that
I was worth it,
worth pushing past
the fear
Alas, you are not mine,
the fantasy is just a
distraction
so I miss the bigger blessing
I will have the love of a lifetime
He will be all mine,
no fear,
All
Mine

BE INQUISITIVE

Be inquisitive
Ask me what I want
Slide your hand
down and around
my inner thigh
Oh!
Right there
Don't care
what others
do or say
They be
wanting
some
anyway

Feel
my tenderness
around the water
starts to flow

Can't get my
mind together
It's Christmas time
Ho! Ho! Ho!

Santa came down
my chimney
with a bag of
gifts to share

He asked me
what I wanted
for Christmas
Don't care,
bad girls
only dare

Slide some oil
to me
Let Rudolph
light the way

'Cause I want
what I got,
making Christmas
everyday
Santa Clause
in my drawers,
laughing
all the way

So when Santa
comes,
my reindeer runs
Inquisition
ends
in great play
Yay! Yay! Yay!

COCOONING

It isn't the
making of love
that's transformative
It's all we do
as a gift
to the soul
of our lover,
Cocooning
with our
other
It's trust,
conversations and questions
asked and unasked,
words spoken,
no sound
It's laughter,
traveling through life's journey,
the pain
of our individual humanity,
thrusting us
into the soul
of our
other
Where the deepening and widening
of who we are
is made greater by
Where We Go
and
Who We Become
inside our personal
chrysalis
for us to love
wholly and free
We, as the caterpillar does,
must digest ourselves,
Release
every enzyme and
dissolve the ego
We cannot love

at the depth of our
soul's purpose
As we exist today,
whole and free, love
requires new parts
new mind
new heart
new hands
new eyes
new feet
new ears
new mouth
Cocooning new parts
come from protein-rich enzymes
Of courage, faith, perseverance and commitment,
desire to move cells,
creating wings for our parts
So now
when we touch,
we are clear that no
other
mind
heart
hands
eyes
feet
ears
mouth
can submerge
the flight of
Our Butterfly
Ours is Intrinsically linked
to the cells of
Only One
We
Did not hatch from our
Cocoon
to be Ordinary
with Anyone

We
Break through
to be
extraordinary
with, for and to
our souls "just one"
This is why our love making
makes no sense
to others
Our parts
are engineered to
pulsate in a rhythm
heard only by
the configuration of our hearts,
ravaged only by our open hands,
seen only with our eyes wide open
"wantingly" listened to by only new ears,
challenged to grow by our new minds,
guided and protected by our new feet
Inspired, giving truth to doubt,
building substance flowing from our new mouths
Black and beautiful,
pushing each other through
the morphing years of our lives
You and I loving:
Aggressive
Assertive
Concupiscent
Rebirth
Protecting this Love
and what our Destiny is Worth
Protein Rich
Courage, Faith, Perseverance, Committed Parts
Transformative,
Coupled Forever,
Cocooned,
Butterfly Hearts

You Walked Up and In

You walked Up and In
to my life
My world has been
shaping and forming
this love
since the day
doctors brought me
from the womb
I mistook others
for my partner,
my best friend
So much distraction,
living without true
intimacy
again and again

You wrapped your soul
around me,
came to my place of
sorrow and grief,
bound me,
no words,
just eyes, hands and legs,
surrounded me
From your
Mamma's womb
came the fruit
for my tree
of life
and I will take in
all its nectar
'cause you
affecting me
like no other
Getting me,
digging deep,

respecting me,
freeing me
To love you,
be in love with you
Together
We Are
From the Womb
to the Tomb
I Do!

ESSENCE

Would you know
me
in different skin

Would the essence
of my
soul
dance in
your spirit
Could I paint
the love
holding court
in your eyes,
the truth
that time
is cruel,
is lonely,
sometimes
selfish

Would you imagine
the possibility,
the strokes
of my brush,
the flick of the
camera,
the rush,
the truth
that love
is breathless,
silent,
a simple smile,
tilt of the head
Sensation is touch
memories,
sweet beginnings,
precious memories

Would you know
me
in different
skin
Where your soul
starts,
ah, one breath,
and my soul
begins

PASSIONS OF THE MIND

From the corner of the room,
I see your body
It stands like a
Monument,
Strong,
Naked
It sends me
into a world
of complete fantasy
That's why you do this to me
I smile
as you walk toward me
I can feel your body
before you arrive
It's like your
sex
is flowing all
over me
I can see this
play in your eyes
One arm
goes around me
The second
takes the back of my head
Oh
don't do that
Now I
want to be
fed

Work that
Black magic
I can feel
you pulsate
inside
From the seconds
in the corner,
to my flesh
now pounding,
there's nothing left to hide
Gently slide
down to it
My mind and body
feel hot
because I think
you like teasing me
Oh my
A new spot
Pressure
is increasing
I think I
want to come
to the place
your body's
moving me
Oh
Wow
Our two
is now
one

YOUR COLOGNE

I smell your cologne
It lingers on my senses for
some time
Can't describe all my
feelings
Some are just too wild
Most think me proper,
professional and poised
I'm all of that and much, much
more
especially when I'm negotiating
with the big boys
But wouldn't they
be amazed
to see me lying here
nude
and in a daze
Touched by love,
gripped by masculinity
All creative with my lover,
re-designing possibilities

Oh wouldn't those boyz
be in shock
to see me
whipped and worked out
Wouldn't they love to know
what gives me the passion
when my gear is in overflow
I have to stop this
He's been gone for hours
but I still feel his kiss
So glad this man loves me,
is marrying me
and setting me free
for this is a passion
we both share
I wonder
what he's smelling
of mine
when I'm not there
When he's not wit' me

MAN IN THE DOORWAY

How do you define sexy?
Well it walked in the door today,
said very little
but everything about him
in that second
made him that way

Not a lot of words,
sometimes talking removes the fun
but if he offered
that conversation
might
be the one

Soft, full lips,
a smile asking me to call,
give me one of those kisses
might be tempted to give my all

Oh, I know he sees me,
knows I'm looking right at him
Oh my, felt a sensation,
thank God
for sexy, beautiful men

Wish he had a moment,
really an hour or two,
'cause I got a lot of imagination,
explore places where words won't
do

Yeah, I want to get to know him,
figure what issues work in his mind,
want to make sure
there's
sustenance to that man,
gotta be more than just fine

So when the conversations are over,
we have laughed, discussed and
debated
I have found a friend
soon to be lover
that makes my
sexiness
overjoyed
and elated

TIME

Time
slipping away from me
but I don't care
'cause you're with me
Nothing matters
except the words
you release
The heat from your body
gives rise to my mind
I know it's all the teasing
'cause my imagination is just fine

Time
slipping away
Let it go, let it go, let it go
There's so much going on here,
your eyes are telling me, so
wrap that love around me
Time gives you a good groove
Just open up to me
Ah ... slight hesitation,
but I knew you would

Time
taking its toll
Gotta be who we really are
Better let you return
This trip took me ... too far
But I'll meet you here tomorrow,
same place -same time
Just bring all your equipment
'cause my imagination
is
just fine

COLLIDE ... EXPLODE

There are no
words
for the tenderness
of your touch

There have been
few men
who gripped the
essence of my being
Who could light
the pathway
to my purpose
Who could bathe
in the aroma
of my majesty
and still
be the man
He
was called
to be

There are few
words
for the depth
of the love
you share

My horizons are
expanded
My love has been
commanded
and I freely
give what makes
me whole

For our destination
has eternity
written across it
For God knew
our souls
played together
in heaven
We were always
the perfect fit

Just had to be
patient,
stop watching the clock
and our aging
for He knows
no date,
just truth as
as we
spin around

Collide
Explode
to create stronger
planets,
bigger stars
Connecting our hearts

'Cause
really
there are
No
Words

WAKE UP WITH ME

Wake up with me
Give me reasons to smile
It gives me memories to
last for a lingering while

I rarely question
the beauty of your soul,
never let you hold back
the mysteries that unfold

Dreaming of what could be
on days you're not with me
sends your aroma
through my mind,
tingles of passion down my spine

I see how you "feel" me
Your eyes,
your senses,
tell no lies
It's all about us,
this ecstasy is going to bust

Like warm running water
cleansing the thoughts within,
can't wait
till tomorrow
to
wake up with you
again

WHAT LOVE DOES

Love
makes room
for
laughter
struggle
joy
family, in and out of "blood"
sickness and health
listening
faith
more lovin'
Love is God's soul,
connecting
two Hearts into
one,
filling the
black hole

FINGERS, HANDS, MOUTH

Do You Remember
my thighs,
the curve
and the dips?
Does the Flames De Amour
still flow slowly
from your lips?

Sitting in Ecstasy
from your deep
penetrating love
What is left...
Our scent hovers
Above
For in the Majesty
of your majestic
comes the moan
and bemoans of long exhales
Fingers, Hands, Mouth
Entering
the Abyss
The hole of our Souls
now free
from passions
Clenched Fist
Do You Remember?

Sister's Wedding

Today,
I walk into my future
My eyes fixed on God
and my heart fixed on you
Today,
I step into a union
with unlimited potential
and endless possibilities
Today,
unlike any other day of my
life,
I know what prayer can do
For God answered my prayer
in the form of you
Today,
prayer
is our protector,
guidance counselor and
friend
Today,
marks the beginning
of a love
that will not end
Today,
is my victory
where partnership
and truth prevail,
where respect is
ever prevalent
and on honor we set sail
Today,
I give you
all that He has made
For in this gift
flows His love,
God's most precious
shade

2:52AM

He Knew
what to do
no words
no touch
those eyes
Sang lyrics to me
body moving
eyes lusting
hands reaching

He Knew
what to do
beckon me
wanting me
recalling me
to a place
Rarely felt
often forgotten
by availability

We Knew
naked in our truth
this depth of connectedness
heightened our
unexpectedness
saturating our thirst
to be each other's
First
and
Only

SEEN THE SUNRISE

I have seen the sun rise
Many years of
my life
I have seen many hearts
bow to a love
they
neither
knew existed
nor
could resist its awesome power
I have been blessed
to love in a way
that makes
My Soul ... Dance,
My Heart ... Race,
My Hands ... Clap,
And
My Spirit ... Soar
This is how I love
Love You
every day and
evermore

I have seen the sun
many years of my
life
yet it has never
shined
more bright
than the day you
agreed
to be
My Partner
My Friend
My Passion
My Soulmate
My Wife

REGRETS

Somehow
I can see you
Just the outline of who you are
Your existence
is my persistence
Because on this journey,
I've come far,
a long road travelled
to place face
and a soul
to make my half
whole
My fingers
want to touch you
My body could
stand the touch
gor there is but one man
who will temperate a rush
So I'll wait
for the Lord
like a painter
waiting to reveal
the entire portrait
When art becomes real,
let not me hurry
for half I may get
I already been through
that
Don't want no more
regrets

WHITE COLLAR & INHIBITED

The strangest thing
is that I like you
You made me laugh
and let go of some tension
Felt like a new born horse
having the fluid of birth
slowly melt away
Got a revived spirit
Your energy was strong
It lingers with me as I write
It adds credence to my thoughts and words
I will use my memories
as another "picture" to draw energy from
You should have more sources to drain from
This writing is dedicated
to your statement
or assessment of me
While I may be white collar
and, okay, sometimes inhibited,
I am also radiating an energy
that gives flight
to your life force – Admit it!
I'm a rocket
with the potential
to surpass the limit,
to reach a place
few are blessed to travel
and to remain centered
because of and with my faith
I am beautiful
but my beauty is internal
The description you gave
is a paradigm
I learned those inhibitions
I can learn to release them

So, my white collar,
non-conformist, easy-going friend,
thanks again
I hope you remain
the gift you are
and I will carry
Friday's events with me
EXCITED
GLOWING
A whole different
Composition
Closer to my wholeness
Releasing all my
Inhibitions

Acknowledgements

The Lord is my shepherd, I lack nothing...

I am grateful! God has been talking to me since I was a child. He continues to whisper WORDS to my soul while reminding me even through the vicissitudes of life, I lack nothing. He gave me the gift of WORDS!

I have not always believed that I lack nothing. Like so many of us, we find our worth in support of family, friends, employers, partnerships and communities. Yet, your true worth cannot be defined by externalities; it is in the simple yet beautiful package called you. My writing has been the blessing, offering a constant way of connecting through grief, loss, love, abuse, ego, image, fear, courage and victory. This book celebrates courage, curiosity and gratitude. By writing and releasing these poems, I trust in my calling and pray I am helping others run toward their healing and wholeness as well. Writing is my brave and safe place of authenticity.

I want to first acknowledge my parents. My soul was born in the care of Charles William (1938-2005) and and Barbara Ann Harris (1941-2017). I grew up in Elizabeth, New Jersey. My parents worked tirelessly for the city they loved. They were funny, compassionate and community focused. They dedicated their lives to making a difference in the lives of others. My father leveraged his gifts through education, being a gifted orator, and politics. My mother leveraged her gifts through her loving heart, ability to galvanize people to perform better and desire for young women to get an education. Collectively, their footprint is forever left in the hearts and minds of generations of people in Elizabeth. There are times when their absence renders me without words... breathless. We were the three amigos. For better or worse, we walked through life together. I miss them in ways words still cannot fully capture. I celebrate their legacy and I am *more than blessed* to be called their daughter.

I grew up with some amazing family members. We shared life experiences, listened to old stories, received excellent advice and guidance from our elders, gained wisdom and learned survival skills over great food and fun. Love, faith, family and history adds to the fabric of my life. I love and miss those of you who have passed on. I celebrate the Harris, Fitch, Leach and Goyins families – my grandmothers, aunts, uncles, sister, brother-in-law, cousins, nieces and nephews. I also recognize those who my parents established as "aunts" and "uncles" by love, not blood. They are my extended family. I am grateful for each of you and love you from the bottom of my heart.

As I write this paragraph of acknowledgements, there are not enough pages to list the names of my friends – friends I regard as family. I begin with my childhood friends who hold such a deep connection to my life and who were my first inspirations for writing at age 8. I count myself extremely fortunate to be called family/sister-friend by those who have walked life's path with me. I have amazing sister- and brother-friends who have made my journey special. These amazing people, at different points along my journey, have been present for moments of great joy, celebration, deep sorrow and life-altering events. I love and appreciate them – family by love and not blood. They are prayer warriors, truth-tellers, mentors, sorority/line sisters, caretakers, survivors, classmates, therapists, poetry book reviewers and people changing the world through their gifts, intelligence and tenacity.

For those who have impacted my life spiritually, I thank God for your ministry and investment in my growth and development. Special acknowledgement to those serving communities in Elizabeth, New Jersey; Detroit, Michigan; Memphis, Tennessee; Somerset, New Jersey; Pittsburgh, Pennsylvania; and Charlottesville, Virginia.

From the bottom of my heart, thank you all! Thanks for loving me and encouraging me. You listened, read, edited, provided feedback and have inspired me for a long time. This is my thank you to God and the gifts He gave me in each of you. Glory to God!

The book would not be possible without two special and gifted people. Thanks to the illustrator, Abraham Yoseff. Thank you for your artistic creativity and your willingness to co-partner with a new author. Your ability to capture words then transform them into art that tells a story is a gift. I am so grateful for you. Thank you, Jasmin Hudson, CEO of Pen & Pad Publishing, for believing in my dream, guiding me, supporting me and having the patience of Jobe. Your partnership over this process has made publishing my first book an educational and joy-filled experience. I look forward to future endeavors. May both of your dreams come true and your businesses prosper.

My heartfelt appreciation to each of you. I did not list names to ensure I did not leave anyone out. Tears are streaming from my face as I think of my parents and each of you. What a journey it has been and what an amazing journey to come! I love each and every one of you. My heart is so full! Who is **More Blessed Than Me?**

> *... He makes me lie down in green pastures,*
> *He leads me beside quiet waters, He refreshes my soul.*
> *He guides me along the right paths for his name's sake.*
> *Even though I walk through the darkest valley, I will fear no evil,*
> *for you are with me; your rod and your staff,*
> *they comfort me. You prepare a table*

before me in the presence of my enemies.
You anoint my head with oil; my cup overflows.
Surely your goodness and love will follow me all the days of my life,
and I will dwell in the house of the Lord forever.
Psalm 23

Contact me at:

www.DaretoBearFruit.com

www.facebook.com/DareToBearFruit

www.instagram.com/DareToBearFruit

www.twitter.com/DareToBearFruit

LAH@daretobearfruit.com

About The Author

LA Harris believes in the power of transformation through the gift of words. Her first poem, at the age of fourteen, was called Camp Goodbye. It was written and read on her last night of Girl Scouts camp. It was in the silence she heard the words pouring into her spirit. She has been moved by the influence words have on minds, hearts, bodies and souls.

Her words celebrate her faith, seek peace, embrace love, question humanity, struggle with doubt and fear, and push readers to think and pursue the possibilities. Her words celebrated weddings and the birth of children, support through sickness, loss and grief, a cheering station for promotions and new opportunities, and a call to justice in places of silence. Her writing has always been to encourage, inspire, to honor and to respect the journey called life, and to thank God for every word breathed onto paper that transformed a moment in time.

She is known to people as a person of faith, academician, a coach, consultant, collaborator, trainer, speaker, passionate, project manager, problem solver, idea generator, consensus builder, and results oriented. She earned her undergraduate degree at Hampton University and her graduate degree at Northwestern University, Kellogg Graduate School of Management. She owns LA Harris Consulting. Her work experiences include Ford Motor Company, American Express, Kean University and University of Virginia.

What is most important to LA is being known as a daughter, sister, niece, cousin, best friend, Soror and servant. In this, her first poetry book, she fulfills a lifelong dream by adding author to her biography.

CPSIA information can be obtained
at www.ICGtesting.com
Printed in the USA
LVHW071452230322
714205LV00009B/460